The Truth George

by Myka-Lynne Sokoloff

Harcourt
SCHOOL PUBLISHERS

Cover: Corbis; p. 6 SuperStock; p. 7 The Bridgeman Art Library, NY; p. 8 Corbis; p. 9 The Granger Collection, New York, SuperStock; p. 10, 11 The Bridgeman Art Library, NY; p. 12-14 Corbis. All other photos ©Harcourt School Publishers. Harcourt Photos provided by Harcourt IPR and Harcourt photographers Copyright © by Harcourt, Inc.

All rights reserved. No part of this publication may be reproduced or transmitted in any form or by any means, electronic or mechanical, including photocopy, recording, or any information storage and retrieval system, without permission in writing from the publisher.

Requests for permission to make copies of any part of the work should be addressed to School Permissions and Copyrights, Harcourt, Inc., 6277 Sea Harbor Drive, Orlando, Florida 32887–6777. Fax: 407-345-2418.

HARCOURT and the Harcourt Logo are trademarks of Harcourt, Inc., registered in the United States of America and/or other jurisdictions.

Printed in Mexico

ISBN 10: 0-15-350278-9
ISBN 13: 978-0-15-350278-1

Ordering Options
ISBN 10: 0-15-349940-0 (Grade 5 ELL Collection)
ISBN 13: 978-0-15-349940-1 (Grade 5 ELL Collection)
ISBN 10: 0-15-357313-9 (package of 5)
ISBN 13: 978-0-15-357313-2 (package of 5)

If you have received these materials as examination copies free of charge, Harcourt School Publishers retains title to the materials and they may not be resold. Resale of examination copies is strictly prohibited and is illegal.

Possession of this publication in print format does not entitle users to convert this publication, or any portion of it, into electronic format.

2 3 4 5 6 7 8 9 10   126   12 11 10 09 08 07

George Washington was born in 1732. He was a leader from boyhood until his death. Many stories and facts about his life show this to be true.

Do you know the story about George Washington and the cherry tree? When George was young, he chopped down a tree without permission. Later, his father asked George who did it. "I cannot tell a lie," said George. "I chopped down that tree."

People have told this story many times. It's a good story, but it is not true. People made up this story to show that George Washington was an honest person.

Rules for Living

In real life, George had strict ideas about how he should act. When George was about ten years old, he copied a list of rules. The list had over one hundred rules about how to behave! The rules taught proper ways to speak and act.

George tried to follow these rules when he was a boy. Many of the rules also guided George when he grew up.

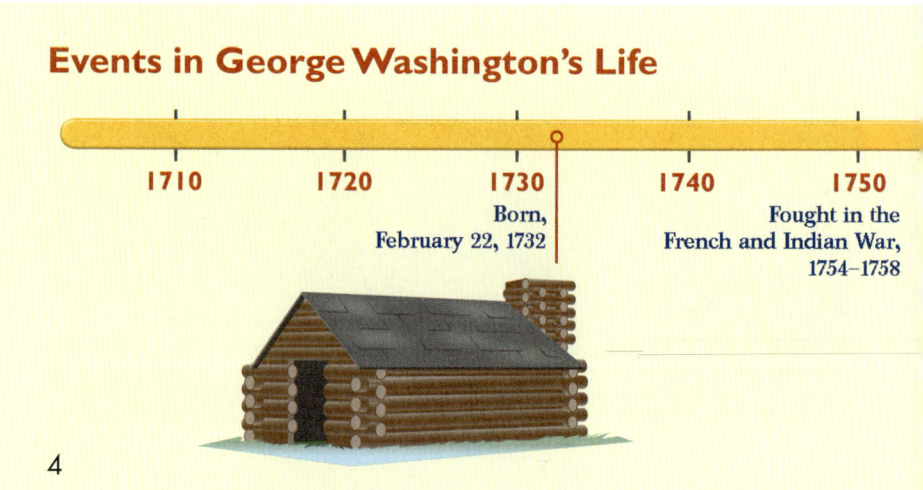

Events in George Washington's Life

1710 — 1720 — 1730 — 1740 — 1750

Born, February 22, 1732

Fought in the French and Indian War, 1754–1758

Sports Lover

When George was a boy, he loved running, wrestling, and other sports. George would line up his classmates and have them march in parades. When the students had disagreements, George decided who was right.

Later, people said that George threw a silver dollar across the Potomac River. This story was supposed to show that George was a great athlete. However, the Potomac River is a mile wide. This story is not true. That event never happened.

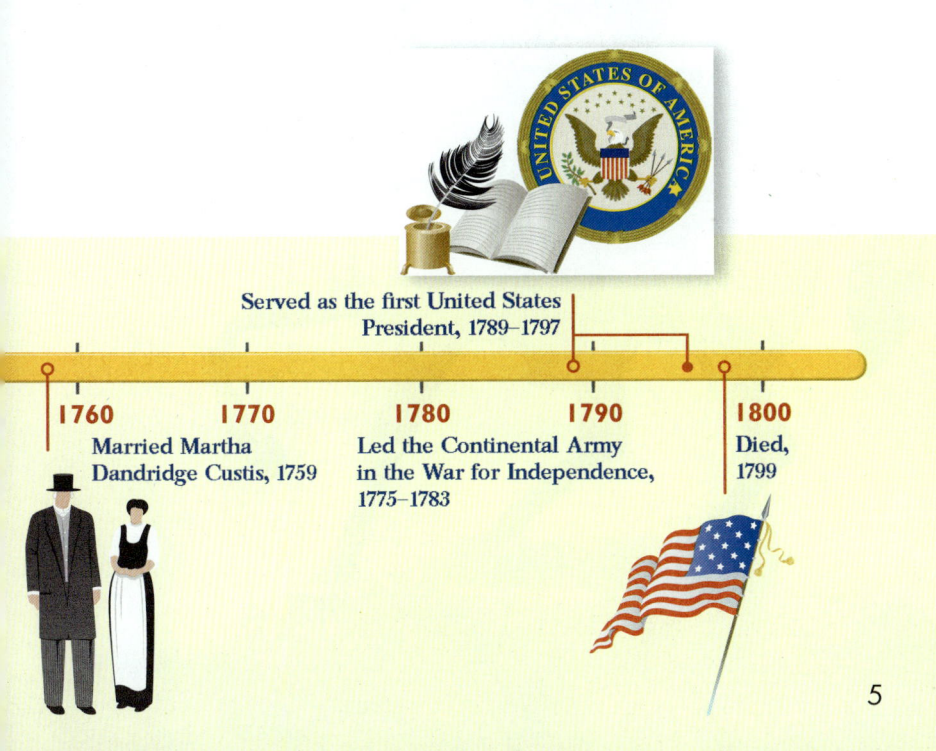

Served as the first United States President, 1789–1797

1760 — Married Martha Dandridge Custis, 1759

1770

1780 — Led the Continental Army in the War for Independence, 1775–1783

1790

1800 — Died, 1799

French and Indian War

George Washington fought in the French and Indian War when he was a young man. The war took place in North America from 1754-1763. That was long before the War for Independence. The colonies still belonged to Great Britain at that time. The colonists and the British fought on the same side in the French and Indian War.

People could always depend on George. George was known for his bravery and honesty. According to legend, in 1758, George was leading some soldiers from Virginia through the woods. The night was foggy. Suddenly, some shots were fired at them. The soldiers with George started shooting, too. Then George saw the people who had fired first. They were part of his army. Friendly soldiers were fighting each other by mistake!

George Washington tried to make the soldiers stop fighting. *Hold your fire!* George tried to shout. No one could hear George's order over all of the noise. George quickly threw himself between the two sides. The soldiers stopped fighting when they saw George in the middle. George's quick thinking saved many lives. George could have lost his own life.

The War for Independence

In 1758, George Washington thought he was done with the army. He returned home to Virginia where he married Martha Custis. George was happy at home with his family.

Then trouble started between Great Britain and the colonies. The colonists decided that they wanted to form their own government. War between Great Britain and the colonies began in 1775. The new government needed someone to lead its army against Great Britain. The army was called the Continental Army. The new government wanted George Washington for the job. George did not want the job. Still, George could not refuse.

Sir William Howe was a British general. General Washington and General Howe were enemies. In 1776, Howe beat Washington at the Battle of Long Island. Washington and Howe would meet again in a few more battles.

One such battle was in Germantown, Pennsylvania, in October 1777. About 1,000 soldiers were killed, wounded, or taken prisoner.

Sometime during the battle, General Howe's dog ran away. Some people think the dog was a fox terrier. Fox terriers are good hunting dogs. Maybe the dog tried to chase after a deer. Maybe the dog was hungry. Perhaps the dog followed the smell of food into Washington's camp.

George refused to take money for leading the army.

Somehow, the dog ended up in the hands of George Washington. Luckily, George was very fond of dogs. Even though George lost the battle to General Howe, he returned Howe's dog when the fighting ended. George even sent a polite note with the dog!

George Washington was very fond of animals. He had many horses and dogs. A few of his dogs were named Lady Rover, Mopsy, Forester, and Captain.

Washington's home, Mount Vernon

The colonists finally won the War for Independence. In 1783, George Washington said good-bye to the army. He was ready to go home. George liked to spend time in his garden. One of George's favorite things was cutting the branches on his fruit trees. (Maybe that story about the cherry tree had some truth to it!)

The country still needed George. A new government was forming. People wanted one person to lead the new country. The colonists wanted a strong leader. The colonists asked George Washington to be the first President of the United States. It's no surprise that the colonists picked George. George had been a great leader in battle. Now people wanted George to lead the country as well.

George Washington agreed to lead the country. The people had long talks about what to call him. Some people wanted to call him *Your Highness*. Later, it was decided to call him *Mr. President*. We still use that name for the President today.

George Washington served as President for eight years. Many people wanted George to stay in office. People thought George should be President for the rest of his life. George was ready to step down, though. George believed his work was done.

In 1796, George Washington finally left the government. George was ready to go home, to tend his garden and play with his grandchildren. People were sad when George left office.

George Washington died in 1799. Thomas Jefferson, our third President, said this about Washington: "He was, indeed, in every sense of the words, a wise, a good, and a great man." Over the years, people have agreed with Jefferson's words. Today George Washington is still a model of honesty and bravery, more than 200 years after his death.

Scaffolded Language Development

PREPOSITIONS Direct students' attention to the time line on page 5 and review the events with students. Write the following sentences on a chart, underlining the prepositions as shown:

> George Washington was born <u>in</u> 1732.
> His birthday is <u>on</u> February 22.
> The French and Indian War lasted <u>from</u> 1754 <u>to</u> 1763.
> The Colonists fought the French <u>for</u> five years.

Point out each underlined preposition and how it is used before a phrase indicating time in the sentence. Then have students complete the following sentences with prepositions:

George Washington got married ____ 1759.
He led the Continental Army ____ 1775 ____ 1783.
Washington served as President ____ eight years.
He died ____ December 14, 1799.

Social Studies

Student Time Line Have students research George Washington on the Internet and write a few facts about the early part of his life. Ask students to share their facts with the group.

School-Home Connection

Family History Suggest that students ask family members to share some family memories and dates. Tell students to say some sentences about these events using prepositions.

Word Count: 1,038